Rico Lebrun Drawings

Foreword by James Thrall Soby

University of California Press
Berkeley and Los Angeles
1968

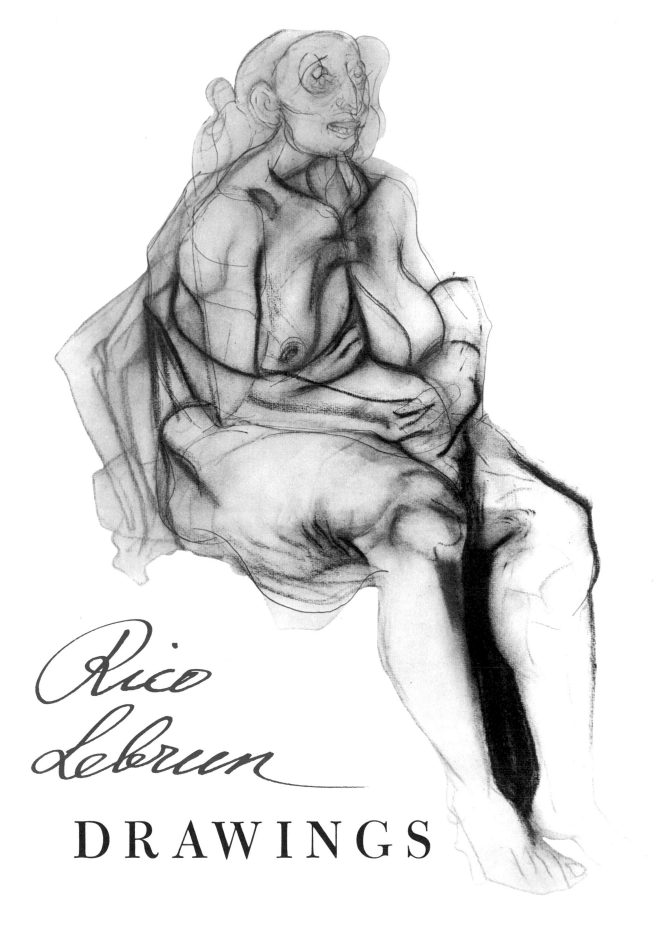

Rico Lebrun

DRAWINGS

University of California Press
Berkeley and Los Angeles, California
Cambridge University Press
London, England
© 1961 by The Regents of the University of California
Second Printing, 1968
Library of Congress Catalog Card Number: 60-16562
Designed by Ward Ritchie
Printed in the United States of America

The photographs of the drawings in this book were taken by the following:
Steve Ballard, Richard Fish, John Mahon,
Barney Burstein, Marcel Ray, and Constance Lebrun.

Foreword

Among American painters of his generation, Rico Lebrun is almost unique in the effulgent certainty of his draftsmanship. In describing his works and aims he uses the word "baroque" often: nowhere, I think, more revealingly than in his eloquent description hereinafter of the city of Naples, where he was born and grew up. He is talking about the Neapolitan crowds, and he says: "From the earliest hour of the day the mob passed to and fro, from the most beautiful of Venuses with Medusa heads to gnomes and monsters—anatomical jokes, obese horrors, angels with mermaid bodies, whose main purpose was to beg, make, or steal enough to survive the day . . . They were a baroque crowd in every sense of the word, and they explained, as no theories of aestheticians can, the baroque idea by living it in the streets."

Lebrun himself has lived the baroque idea rather than merely adopted its art-historical premise. With his talents he could easily have let grand-style drawing relapse into virtuosity. On the contrary, his passion for dramaturgy and for exploring it both in the life around him and in man's cultural and religious heritage has been committed and unrelenting. In this he has been deliberately unfashionable and stood aloof from schools of painters. He has been a maverick to whose lonely ear violence speaks with a particular urgency. The more distraught charades of our civilization have appealed to him especially. Consider, for example, some of the subjects of his art: the West's slaughterhouses; the contortions of rotting machinery and of cripples fleeing air raids; turtles and soldiers perplexed and lumbering in their armor. As in the graphic art of Goya, whose example has recurred to Lebrun over the years, the imagery the latter proposes is more often motivated by fervor than by calm, by feverish emotional involvement rather than esthetic autonomy. Lebrun strikes hard and fast with the sharp blade of his extremely personal conviction. His protests against mankind's brutality are never overly satirical, but they remain a terrible indictment of those whose cruelty, dissemblance, and corruption have caused the scars of this and earlier times.

As a draftsman Lebrun works within the two traditional extremes of linear precision and bold shading. From the mid-1930's date his first truly mature works such as the Figure in Dust Storm *(pl. 1), succeeded during the ensuing decade by drawings which gradually move away from the classicism of* Portrait of Kate Lawson *and* Clown *(pls. 3, 5) to the neo-baroque eloquence of* The Ragged One *and* Woman Leaning on a Staff *(page 7, pl. 7). And then, in 1948, he began the voluminous series of drawings which led up to his immense triptych of the* Crucifixion, *completed in the winter of 1950–51. These drawings, notably those entitled* Woman of the Crucifixion, *are literally breathtaking in their assurance and power, and it is heartening to know that some of the finest are now to be reproduced in the pages of this book. In our era, to treat so sacrosanct a subject, to be unafraid of restating its grandeur in modern terms—this took courage of a high order and profound sensitivity and skill. Lebrun himself has explained his decision: "My choice of the theme, Crucifixion, was prompted by the constantly repeated history of man's blindness and inhumanity. My painter's language is founded on the belief of a traditional function of art, that is, to communicate, through dramatic presentation, a legend; a story." That Lebrun was equal to the exalted task he had set himself will, I think, be clear in the plates which follow.*

The Crucifixion *finished, Lebrun went to Mexico for a year and a half, from late 1952 until mid-1954. While there, the theme of the Crucifixion continued to haunt him for a time, and on it he based several large and relatively abstract collages, the finest of which, alas, was disassembled when he left Mexico, though a photograph has survived (pl. 29). On his return to this country, his compassionate horror at mankind's ordeals focused on the German concentration camps of World War II, and he completed in charcoal on canvas such large-scale works as the* Buchenwald Pit *(pl. 30), wherein strewn anatomical fragments summarize the mad butchery of the Nazi jailors. Perhaps his absorption in wartime carnage turned his mind again to Goya, for there followed the series of drawings he calls* Goyescas, *its climax reached in the altogether aston-*

Foreword

vi

ishing and beautiful Familia Real (*pl. 39*). *To make this sort of original and penetrating commentary on the style and iconography of a predecessor in the history of art is a very considerable achievement indeed. Lebrun's gifted hands allowed him to arrive at a monumental lyricism instead of at pastiche.*

During the academic year 1958–59 Lebrun became a visiting member of Yale University's art department. His teaching duties did not prevent him from drawing incessantly, as he has done throughout his distinguished career, and he produced such admirable works as the Sitting Nude, Two Standing Figures, Casualties *and* Standing Figure (*title page, pls. 50, 51, 58, 56*). *At this juncture he was much preoccupied with broadening the intervals between component parts of his compositions. "I had been crowding my figures too much," he told me recently. Remembering the mastery of his previous drawings, it may be difficult for the observer to understand why he should have been troubled by spatial problems. Yet it must be said that his research on these problems has given his draftsmanship a heightened freedom and sweep. To which may be added that like most true artists Lebrun goes on learning steadily. He has known a very great deal about drawing since the beginning of his career. Today the unwavering probity of his intelligence has further increased the esteem in which many of us have held him for a long time.*

JAMES THRALL SOBY

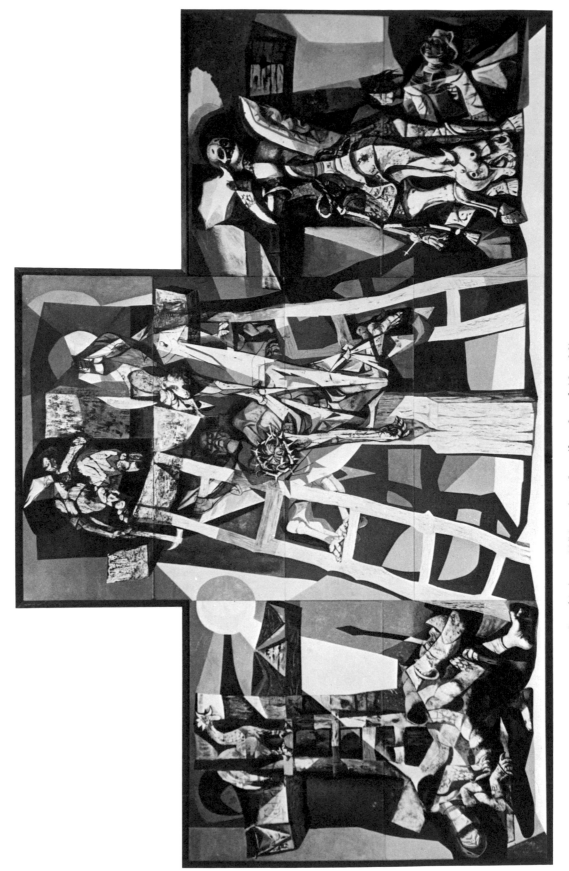

Crucifixion 1951 triptych oil on board 16 x 26'
Donated by the Whitney Foundation in 1957 to Syracuse University.

Contents

About Myself

About Myself

You will say, Why not let someone else write for you? It is embarrassing to speak for yourself and to explain. Far less, I can answer, than to have myself explained through the words of another. In the end, except for the shape of our nose, and the size of shoe we wear, all of it is fiction, a will to be so and so in such and such a way. And even the shape of our nose and the size of shoe can be misrepresented by vanity. All of it to me is fiction, and I would rather make and buy my own fiction than to have to blush at the consequences of another man's.

3

Legends are cheap, and I am not one to buy my own second hand; in fact at times not even first hand. Yet I believe one can tell more, and more truthfully, in fiction, and this is because I have often made —by anticipation or wish and following action—fiction into the facts of painting. Above all, I believe there is a limit of decency to personal revelation, a limit respected only by the rare biographers who are chroniclers and not mongers. I want to see to it that these notes be not in the nature of holy truculence or irascible bore, or the utterance of the partisan or the lone man. I am essentially none of these things. Truculence and ire bore me. And I have seen writers turn the essentially modest figure of an artist into a Procrustes or a Hamlet or a defender of the faith; I have seen them burden him with ridiculous roles he could not sustain for long. And when the artist finally crumbled, the writers, the crocodiles, who can grieve so gleefully, wrote the obituary.

The real drama is in the fact that personal drama produces nothing of merit whatever. Many professors have struggled even harder than Cézanne, and for the wrong reason. In a superior civilization some day, we should have a Pantheon for them. "He was an ass and toiled as if he had the obligations of a hero." Who knows how many of us may yet belong to that legion?

I have unshaken admiration for the dry-eyed performance which is, so to speak, on the level, and refuses to lean in any way whatsoever on the dramatics of daily misfortunes. Let this be our quiet secret; let this be decently kept in check from interfering with other fundamental issues of validity and pertinence. Particularly in the case of the artist with a preference for the dramatic or tragic statement, it is proper and decent that he reserve his energy and eloquence for the statement itself, refraining from turning to the audience in public or private, calling it to bear witness to his personal agitation, which is part and parcel of his privilege to be a creator, and should be taken silently and liberally with several grains of salt.

All things being equal, it should make no difference to the reader how many times I fail before I succeed; no difference except to me, of course, and to me failure means that I have been too conceited for veracity, too obtuse for the job at hand, or too profound to let well enough alone, or an embroiled mixture of the three. Of certain I know that the revisions that come to the mind and hand of an artist through failure are at times revelations to himself, hints of what he should be at all times but is not, except in the briefest of flashes. To prepare carefully the terrain for these brief moments is to plan a strategy which can only be written on paper but not acted upon, because the man we are working with is recalcitrantly dedicated to the unglorious business of keeping alive from day to day. I for one do not consider myself a campaign for success; not even a shot gun; at most the assorted and scattered ammunition rattling at the bottom of the box with the chewing gum, the broken cigars, and the hunting license. The last item is most important. Certainly, before we even talk about these things, we should make sure that we are licensed for the hunt. Arabia Deserta, Lawrence said, is not a terrain for children.

Naples, where I was born at the beginning of this century between the first and second Italian colonial wars and before the First World War, was a town of dream and delight and also of sordid life. A town

Lebrun

4

of abysmal darks and dazzling lights like a huge vat in constant fer
ment, a total anatomy in frantic, comical, extravagant gesturing. In
speech and singing alike, it had a voice pitched higher than necessary
for common speech, raucous and, if you can imagine the combination,
melodious at the same time. There were songs about a head of lettuce
which sprouted overnight in the middle of the bay; the Turks, according to the song, were fighting over it with scimitars. Another song told
of the black fish which ordered a suit of scales and seaweed and went
looking for a wife. Another, which we sang as children, interceded with
the moon to send down no more heavenly gift than a plate of lasagne,
warning that if it were poor in condiment it would be smashed back
into the moon's face. Another had words, which I can only surmise as
Greek, that spoke of beheaded saints.

The game of survival, hard pushed by want, gave the people that
bright, bitter face which is truly, without wanting to stress pathos,
constantly between sobbing and laughter. Off and on we lived near
the center of the Section of the Stars, in a house twenty steps away
from the Church of the Sanità, a rusty cake of a building whose inte-
rior walls were hung with crutches and rifles and ex-votos from the
survivors of the massacre at Addis Ababa. At every dawn our street,
like all others, slowly emerged from visceral darkness into peach-and-
brass light, shrouded in miasmic smells and heavenly fragrances, fes-
tooned by immaculate laundry hanging everywhere on lines like angels
electrocuted in the sun. From the earliest hour of the day the mob

passed to and fro, from the most beautiful of Venuses with Medusa heads to gnomes and monsters—anatomical jokes, obese horrors, angels with mermaid bodies, whose main purpose was to beg, make, or steal enough to survive the day. They had ways which of course I learned well but which would surprise the stranger. Adamant about trifles to the point of revenge, they considered the major and serious aspects of honor as being negligible nonsense. Truly indomitable, they relished the role of victims only to pity you with laughter and suddenly become Spartans if you pitied them. They would volunteer complex fabrications in answer to the most innocent question. Half naked, they had a superb gift for shrewd reserve and for obscuring the tracks of the most evident issues. They were a baroque crowd in every sense of the word, and they explained, as no theories of aestheticians can, the baroque idea by living it in the streets.

Lebrun

6

In the tide of all this, in the full sight and sound of this, one either yells or chokes. As for me, I had either to draw or to wither. I think I took to the baroque notion long before I saw it in the museums. My forms were about all this. Whenever I have abandoned the kinship with its essence, I have produced aesthetic exercises. Whenever I have tapped it at the core, I have felt real. Even today the thing I like best next to drawing, and which I do with incredible zest and relevance, is to fill page after page with sentences in my native dialect when I want to remind myself of things I wish to do in my art, to recapture and certify qualities which I relate to drawing and expression. Its words are full and continuous, yet unexpectedly broken by syncopation and truncated by mute finals; accented, fast, and direct, these words must be written black and firm—sometimes, to make them even more so, I rewrite the phrase. More than any other speech I know, they fit meaning like a glove, which is what I want drawing to do.

The ugliest drawings I have ever seen were probably done in the Accademia di Belle Arti, where I attended night classes. The school, in the true conservative tradition, kept itself carefully isolated from the stream of life around it. A frigid sort of neoclassicism was the rule within its walls. Laboring endlessly over fixed poses and plaster casts, the pupils produced horribly competent renderings. My own performances were, according to the minds in power, so deficient that soon I found myself at the tail end of the class. In desperation I went

to the museum, where I could study the facsimiles of the old masters in the library. Thus in a quiet way I had my own private revolution. I mean to say that at least I went from the dead to the living.

The few adult painters I knew at that time were all engaged in a form of impressionism which I could not reconcile with either the tone or the character of the life around me. The adopted confetti color ill suited the carnal and tangible quality of the town, which in fact only baroque masters of southern Italy had previously understood. These painters (my contemporaries) considered themselves radicals for having adopted the bright tonality of French impressionism. Probably to them these values meant those of enlightenment. The result, however, had the effect of putting a blazer on the back of a bull.

If the artistic milieu was a desert, the intellectual life of the town was intensely alive. Among teachers at the university, friends of my father, and youngsters only a few years older than myself, the pupils and partisans of Aquinas, Vico, Campanella, Croce, and De Sanctis kept alive the regal mobility of mind which distinguished the south in the story of our Italian culture. This is the song without guitars which upsets all convenient picturesque definitions of us as a race of unfortunate vocalists and nothing more. Elegance and toughness of mind were part of the distinction. I was fortunate in that I could be on the fringe and gain the friendship of some of these men.

Perhaps the most memorable thing about the town had to do with the people themselves. Once a year, for instance, in the Cathedral of

San Gennaro they gathered to witness the miracle of the liquefaction of the blood of the saint. Violently contested and questioned by the unbelievers and the reasoners, and defended, to say the least, ferociously by the crowd in the streets, this event was a shaking and impressive one. From early in the morning in the vast church jammed with human beings, the intercessors—that is, the self-elected relatives of the saint—prayed and begged to his name that the miracle would take place. The petrified blood which was displayed in a flask was believed to liquefy as a sign of benevolence and protection from the patron saint. Failures in the past had always been related to subsequent earthquakes and disasters. The chorus of invocations increased steadily, and to be in the midst of this latent explosion was a frightening and awesome experience. When the miracle happened it was like being on the inside of a clanging bell.

Lebrun

This collective and fierce will, convinced that it could change the inert into the alive, has never been to me a lost lesson. The miracle was that dead matter gave way to faith triumphant. Which goes for painting also.

8

A great deal of what I did then has been destroyed or has disappeared. Apart from the fact that my work at that time pointed vaguely the way I have followed since, it seems of no relevance now. It was, moreover, work interrupted by a prolonged military service beginning toward the end of the first World War, interrupted by the armistice and the subsequent peace, resumed for two more years when my class which had previously been called for war emergency had to serve its regular time. Soon after becoming a civilian again, I became employed in a stained-glass factory.

What I have kept is of more recent years. I show some of these drawings, having been encouraged to do so, more to tell where I have been than to imply how gloriously I was there. I have destroyed hundreds of them and if not restrained would go on doing so until only half a dozen would be left. Such strict editing, however, would be as extravagant as lack of discrimination. Tracing a few steps to tell where I came from seems necessary, but I am in truth no more interested in these drawings than a mule in his own footprints.

I hope this indifference to past results will not be taken as a pose. It seems to be a necessary ingredient in the story of many artists I know today. Reflection leads most of us to decide that we were not so good as we thought at the time.

In 1924 the stained-glass factory secured a contract in the United States. Our new location was in Springfield, Illinois, where I worked as foreman for a year. Subsequently I moved to New York to find my own way. In those days it was relatively easy to get jobs in advertising and illustration; in fact, soon I had to spend most of my time doing commercial art. After a couple of years, being more at ease, I resumed drawing and painting in spite of constant interruptions. This went on until 1935 when I applied for, submitting drawings done in this hecitc period, and won a Guggenheim Fellowship. Soon I received a Treasury Department commission to do a fresco in the New York Post Office Annex. This was my breaking point with commercial art and, like many other painters who worked on government projects, I found the experience helpful as a foundation for moving on independently as a painter. In 1937 I went to Santa Barbara and became a California resident. Soon after I arrived in Santa Barbara, Donald Bear became director of the new museum. He was an exceptional man, and his encouragement to me at that time was invaluable.

To this early California period belong many portrait drawings as well as the slaughterhouse drawings and paintings. I would say that California, the land and the life, gave me the first true chance to bring drawing closer to objects and people outside the studio. I worked at the drawings in a slaughterhouse for many months, and the experience— of form revealed in movement on a stage which was constantly changing because of the phases of the work—has remained invaluable as a lesson in structural animation. Later, the discovery of agricultural implements was also (as I see it now) of immense help to my painting. Previously my work had been essentially linear, and I was now impatient with the isolation of objects and figures divorced from surrounding space. Time and again, in painting and drawing alike, I had found that the figures and the objects were not properly contained and extended in space. Now the farm machinery had a quality of opened and colored structure, exactly what I had been looking for. Here I found expression in the new sense I needed. The expression was the structure; the interval, the span, was the physiognomy and the countenance. The machinery had square eyes of cobalt and ribs of cadmium red. The open works of the tractor were organs with clangor of orange blood; in the intervals of the open cage, in the furrow of the groin, sprouted the erect, green hair of the buttercup and the sage. The seeding and planting machines were made in the likeness of the locust and the mantis—savage, alert, predatory. The disk harrows were vertebrate; so was the bone-white, upright structure of the axle and wheel. It was here that I also found the world of color that I understand best—color which is the story of the object. A red, damaged and made particular by use; the conditional, the related; the blaze made living and pertinent by sustained function—not the insipid, abstract birthday card, but the temperature chart of fevers and bleedings and rain and droughts. The concept of red in the absolute I understand, but it is finally tiresome because of its anti-human consistency to the index red. Different, more aloof temperaments may care for such notions, but a poor red, a fortunate red, a cruel red are another and, certainly to me, a greater thing.

There came a time when I needed a subject, a theme, which could be put through successive illustrative variations, as a break from the self-centered procedure into which events and personal reverses had cornered me. The choice was a natural one. When I abandoned in my youth, with a sudden revulsion, some things related to my former faith that I could not properly understand, I abandoned at the same time what that faith had of sustenance and clarity. Now, as an outcome of the war years, images related to the Crucifixion began to crowd in upon me in chains of ideas—not scattered thoughts, but a rosary, as it were, of meditation. In a way they were like a commentary on the nature of the Cross, the implements, and the actors.

Lebrun

10

This was a period in which I could go from one picture to another as a speaker goes from one phrase to another—the wood of the Cross, the ladder, the signs, the nails, the hammer, the uniforms of slaughter, the black of mourning. I think it was Melville who had given me courage to do this when he wrote about the spade, the lance, the tow-rope.

I worked a great deal then, as you can do only on a set theme, absolved from the obligation to find a new fact, a new subject every day. This cancels the tragedy of the blank canvas and relegates it to the realm of ridiculous dilemmas, for day and night you are involved in a theme and its variations. Of course you pay for this. The links in the rosary are sometimes weak; but because they are, you should not forgo the opportunity of sustained prayer. My work at this time was not a depiction of the event, in the sense of illustration, but was related to the life and changes of forms and colors, as actors transmuted by the happenings. This all had to do with the world of peace and dream interrupted by sinister slaughter, flaring and hiding, evident and hard to explain at the same time. As events had troubled the face of the earth, so did I now feel the need to trouble the plane of the picture. Far more than for aesthetic effects I worked for psychological meaning. The steps of the ladder of the Cross must have been hard ones to climb; so my rendering had perforce to be hard to read, uneven and obscure. Likewise, I wanted to paint the closeups of the other implements with which I started the cycle (shroud, hammer, nails) in the nature of an apparition. So it was also with the figures of the crying women and the sleeping soldiers, whom I saw as nocturnal structures here and there revealed by light.

The large tryptich which concluded the cycle was executed in six weeks. My assistants and I faced a technical problem, because it was impossible to assemble the tryptich—it was painted in sections—in its entirety in the space we had in the studio. We solved this problem with the help of photographic montage scaled to a smaller version which we would report to the final painting. Our calculations proved correct, because there was not a single change to be made when the work was finally shown in the Los Angeles County Museum and we could see it in its entirety. Needing a medium which would dry fast because of my way of quickly and repeatedly reworking a picture, I was at this time using lacquers. I found them enormously resilient and alive as a medium. Relatively new in the equipment of the painter of today, these lacquers have not been given enough time to prove their worth as a lasting medium. My works of this period have undergone no change whatsoever and have held up well.

Lebrun

12

This brings me to the point of clarifying certain aspects of technique which are related to what I do. Although I consider permanency an important factor, my paramount concern is of course that of expression. Whatever means bring it about, without impediment, serve me best. An exaggerated solicitude for durability would not have made possible the technique of collage, for instance, essentially perishable but fundamentally of great meaning in our time. Likewise, mediums which curtail the slow elaboration of oil paint seem to me to relate perfectly to the character of execution most of us use. If a choice must be made between durability and spiritual pertinence, no painter worth his salt would hesitate in favor of the latter. Above all, I believe that if a potent image later suffers great changes (such as darkening or peeling), the important thing is that it was made to exist. Pigment may darken, glue may crack, paper may not last, but nevertheless ideas will retain their legendary permanence. To me the technical means are put in operation simply as a proposition of give and take. Once they have been drafted to serve a purpose, they have to do the best they can to meet the situation. They may serve with honor or with dishonor. But beyond a certain point of basic decency, I feel that I for one would rather proceed at a gallop so as not to chill than to stop and freeze in favor of a crafty move for the sake of technical prudence.

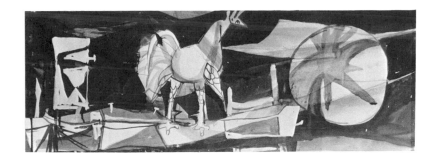

After the period of the *Crucifixion* I moved toward establishing a more intimate contact with the object. Thus followed a long span of time in which I worked on enlarging common things and everyday, obtainable patterns. I reduced the obstacle of the medium to a minimum. With diluted ink on brown paper I painted the X ray of leaves, the veined core of rock. These became other things also: hearts and lungs of creatures of whose total structure I had yet no idea. I do not believe I have ever tried to be more at one with the palmistry of the object. Yet these things are the ones which have seemed to others most difficult to read and most unreal. It was as if I were trying to find the organic module for a new figure and landscape. I was quite happy at this. I had a sense of belonging, of being connected with the mystery of facts. Yet soon I was troubled. There is unquestionable integrity in a black web as the core of a leaf, or in a honeycombed chamber that can stand for head or eye or heart. But here the inventory seemed too narrow. I began to think that, revealing as it may seem, this mode should include not the minimum but the readable section of the forest, the variation of the many leaves. And so also the landscape: it should be readable as a ribbed and sustained geography in which one can walk with a traveling mind. And so the entire figure. The forest and the total anatomy of a being would have to be the subject, and possibly the cry of the animals and the beating of the heart. These were new words I was making, better than many others I had used, more apt, truer. Yet only too rarely would a whole phrase stagger across the page. Mostly they were just words, not speech.

One should not be so unfair and so stupid as to ask a man who is fumbling with new words to write a fragment of the *Odyssey*. But of course I am at liberty to be unfair and demanding of myself. Soon I was asking precisely that. And this was not all impossible presumption. It had to do with the fact that the condensed, the cryptic, in their unassailable brevity, seemed to beg excuse from grosser and vaster commitments. For a moment I realized with panic that I was playing the limited, laconic hand which has made so many careers an original success. "The less you encompass, the better for you." The ampler, I said to myself, pays with the fact that there is more to fail about. The stricter, on the other hand, can be more easily sanctified. A narrower conscience can escape more rain. The strategy of how much not to say is as shallow as the frontal attack of vociferation. They both can make careers; neither is worth a damn, because they are planned sanctity and rehearsed passion.

So, in spite of the jolt, I was happy to come face to face with the fact that the solitary cryptogram, trying to look demure and unassumingly profound, is not enough. I found it wanting in scope of engagement. Therefore the strict diet began to pale and lose credit with me. I am, I realized, on the side of the omnivorous, and I will take the consequences. To want to include too much is for me. It leads to surprises and to unscheduled blood changes. It may also lead any day into, beside vomiting, the most extraordinary complications of the senses at the risk of being redundant and ludicrous. Also it may possibly lead to the increase of my own being and of the forms that are mine. I am for the raucous, long song, not the single, unassailable note, which can be profound if left alone but will not serve in the world of conditional sacrifices that is the composition.

The maps of defeat are at best of pathetic interest. It matters not a jot that today they are so often sanctified by fashion in the name of action painting. I suspect that in their solicitude to avoid the ascertainable they are at best statements about cancelling of statements. Doubt and boredom do the same thing to the speech of the dandy. If at this point one should say that, for instance, any fragment of the *Quinta del Sordo* of Goya's makes abstract expressionism look like a sometime thing, one would immediately be accused of the aficionado's regret for the safe past and be reminded that we are in a historically different situation, "unprecedented" and ahead of Goya. Yes, ahead, and several miles below.

Lebrun

14

At the time of first extended visit to Mexico, the notion of seeing the human figure with a newness and freshness of sensation started haunting me.

As I had anticipated, Mexico was like southern Italy. The presentiment of how the human figure would be revealed—less standardized, less cellophaned, less packaged—proved to be true. Life in Mexico, as physical, immediate revelation, opened up to me. It offered itself without smiling back. But I could look directly in.

Going to Mexico was thus a sort of homecoming. In spite of the tremendous differences between the two peoples, both Mexicans and Italians are penetrable. You can see through them, they reveal themselves, they accept or reject in alternation you and the world around them with a tremendous resiliency, with passion. Their traditional notion of gusto could be more truly called the hunger to be alive. I felt that I was going back to a mode of human operation to which I was accustomed. So I participated in the life around me in ways I had almost forgotten in the more conventional surroundings of the States. In Mexico, in a savage and grand way, I found again things I knew from the land of my birth. The same force seems to shape the face of the landscape and humans alike. I am thinking particularly of the volcanic land and the mountain plateaus of both countries. A fractured quality reveals the outer and inner surface of the land and beings at once. Over and above the surface of the picturesque is the story of colored form with numberless footnotes of phenomenal accidents, bearing the signs of vicissitude, the anticlinical, the acceptance of ravages without palliative of plaster or explanatory consolations. Even the new walls have this obsessive insistence from pebbles to boulders as a petrified explosion. And the new colors are only a transparent skin over the organic body of structure you can easily guess and read through.

In the countryside, defense and offense are relentlessly present in the thousand defensive forms of plants, traps of thorns, and in the unwalkable, cupped erosion of the mud flats, the stony fields, the fissured milpas. Everywhere, everything is fleshless and explained but not habitable or reconciled to you. I always felt that the land could not be surprised by a look. No, it would not stare back. It would stare past you, literally over your head. The distinct, the determinate, the cleansed, and the cellophaned give way to the hybrid, the involved, the indiscriminate, and the multiple.

This is what I had to work with, and I had to stop for a long time and for a long look. And when I began to work again I was satisfied to bring back with me to the studio pieces of day-by-day vision, fragments in the shape of a candy stick, or wounds, or cantaloupe-colored water, or the hand of a doll, or a votive leg. One day all I could obtain was a strip of paper banded in the color of *dulces*, the peppermint, the homicidal pink. Another day, a slab of paper, torn and quartered, barred with white ribs, cloudy with black specks of flies, streaked with crimson, with the plumed pennant of a tail, the *toro muerto*, the bull meat. Another, the coffee-chocolate-ivory-violet lining of a serape. Another, a beggar's armpit, deep as a crater, a lice nest, the meeting point of pulleys, tendons, and ropes to make the imploring gesture possible. And notes, drawings, of heads, arms, torsoes, so evidently declaring their function. A quality of sustained and continuous anatomy related the loincloth wrapped around the pelvis to the swirl of torrents around boulders; the scapular ledge of the rock continued into the heaving rib cage of the sun-bronzed human standing against it. This quality of the revealed body repelled all easy ways of delineation. To render it meant to envelop it with one's understanding made into a line.

In looking over my work when I came back from Mexico, I could see that, rather than being single and, so to speak, formally presentable images, they made sense only when viewed in totality as a

Lebrun

dialogue carried on from day to day. This dialogue was about the remembrance of things and was not a transcription from the factual. Successive siftings of facts through memory produced now and then a glimpse of the reality I wanted.

This had to do with the sum total of remembered and fleeting sensations permitted to appear and finally to fuse themselves into the monumental. Completely antidecorative in purpose, I hoped and still hope that it would lead me into a splendor of sustained arabesque comparable to the handwriting of some of the great wall images I had admired. It was of course no longer actual Mexican geography or general human anatomy that I had in mind, but a new total form, changing from figure to figure even within the framework of one canvas. In the large, now destroyed, Mexican Crucifixion collage, I put some of these notions to work.

I found that collage was of the greatest help to me. As a medium I think it is a world complete unto itself. It permits changes—not just mendings—but true changes; it allows a pacing of growth so rapid that its sum total retains the live face of the unexpected which I find necessary to any image. Because I worked on a large scale, some of these collage assemblies could only be photographed and then disassembled before I left Mexico. I could not avoid thinking at the time, as I saved some of the important sections, how this procedure was like the disbanding of an orchestra, like the packing of the musical instruments. This medium was, in short, a logical part and parcel of the revision of my own values I so much needed at the time. Working in such a frame of operation, which promotes crises as readily as it does solutions, one may naturally come to indulge in sheer histrionics. But ultimately the structure has to reach that fine balance of the transistory, poised and arrested, that coherence of assembly which, if corrected again in the smallest fragment, would again be undone. This balance can happen only when the time is right. Meanwhile some of the most important phases of our labor are precisely those which, while giving the general impression of elaborate vagueness, prepare us for those climactic moments. With me the operation works as follows: if the poetic idea and the structural concept are alive, I feel that I would miss a tremendous amount of meaning in my existence by narrowing down too soon to the direct statement. Directness which is the outcome of many stages is an altogether different thing. For this I, and many painters I respect, mistrust the touch of those who seem to know at all times exactly what they are doing. These men are perhaps the wiser strategists, but to my mind they suffer from the strictures of purity. It is fine to have your own receiving and sending set in perfect order, but the same code day after day must bring a boredom I could not endure. Nor am I here speaking of sheer love of novelty. With me, in spite of the different aspects of my search, the goal is always that of transforming the organic quality of nature. And I can find what I need only by tapping the image on different levels.

This was particularly true of the Buchenwald cycle on which I started working in 1954. Before painting the several versions of the *Pit*, *Buchenwald Cart*, and other related themes, I did many precise and lucid drawings using the photographic documentation available on the subject as a test to maintain and amplify if possible the authenticity of brute fact. Yet after having gone through days of absorbed and almost hallucinatory recording of these awesome fragments, I remember wanting to brush the whole thing away from me: the draftsman made their sight unbearable to me as a man—a just price to pay. Afterward, the mind drifted for a while and then remembered something that was left at its bottom, remembered the upheaval of the spent furnace with fragments, islands here and there, of what had been the living body. Going to work again, I painted several versions, the truest being the ones in which I could not name the islands— pelvis, skull, whatever they had been. So the changes were part of the

Lebrun

18

search to find at which degree the commemoration would read truest. The technique had to be that which answered these requirements precisely; and, in a total revulsion against craft and skill, I found that I wanted to speak out in a single shout. It did not matter to me (and never will) if I permitted the shape of vision to change from day to day. I am confident enough in my own substance to resist incantation of self, and to know that I can operate with the only form of consistency which really matters—the living, breathing chain of daily inconsistencies whose sum total alone can produce design, against arrangements, against vanity.

19

Of one thing I was now sure: the subject was our duplicate and mirror, and I wanted to give shape to that allegiance for me and the spectator to remember. Also I wanted to remember that our image, even when disfigured by adversity, is grand in meaning; that no brutality will ever cancel that meaning: painting may increase it by changing what is disfigured into what is transfigured.

Notes on Drawing

Horsemen in Cemetery, 1957   Lebrun
                                                                              1957

Notes on Drawing

BEGINNINGS

We leave the live center of the human image on the day of our birth, and are after that strangers to its meaning. One of our strongest longings is, nevertheless, to return to that center. But of all human efforts to be included in and to include the mother figure, drawing is perhaps one of the grandest and most real. First and foremost comes the identification with the freight of flesh, the weight of bone, its width and its many depths, with the mechanics of organs, with the form which is us. This hunger precedes the aesthetic act; without it the drawn image cannot live. True, wit and whim can go a long way toward imitating its surface, and we all have had our share of such effects; but they produce neglible results. Revelations are another matter entirely, and there have been very few in the world of drawing of the corporeal; outlines and manners, yes, but seldom the authentic birth cry, the exclamation of surprise of drawing coming to life.

I use a line, I suppose, as a lifeline to hang on to against the risk of being washed overboard and below into the pool of general confusion. Drawing is to me a blessed *yes* to many things which call me, count on me, hold me, and believe in me; it is also a weapon against many other things which could vilify and shame me if I had no means of defense. Someday when I understand many more things than I do now, the fundamentals of my drawing will be so tightly woven into those of existence that I will easily and naturally find the design which is the answer to many questions. Meanwhile I draw continuously. It

23

is difficult for me to renounce drawing for any length of time. I work on, waiting for the fusion of self and ink which is like the nod of him who has fully understood.

DRAFTSMAN AND SUBJECT

To understand means to look. To *look*. No one can say precisely what the aspects of nature mean to a man who is trying to find forms for his own vision. Sight, relentlessly in search of truth, is a taskmaster. The comforts and delights of normal views of the landscape and the figure are constantly crossed by this hunger for unfolding their meaning, for making them come to poetic surrender, to assume poetic form. In the act of drawing, the more or less acute character of this struggle is not always on a par with the forms which come to light. As a consequence of the most grandiose overtures, meaningless and vapid forms will often appear; terrible, true, impressive ones breeze in at other times, easily and without effort. These are the ones which take pity on the bruised apprentice, the artist.

Things are not at all interested in the results of our fumbling, but we can question them so they will answer. In a true dialogue between the draftsman and the unyielding object, the line in response will totter and flash across the page from one point of attack to another, reach the edge of form like an out-of-breath swimmer who has more despair than strength in his stroke. The page looks ridiculously alive and you breathe deeply, as you do after having had a hell of a scare and now it is over. If you manage to look beautiful in this position, that is a fortunate coincidence—almost not your fault.

There is a point past which the human image refuses to play ball. Its structure has a terrible lack of acquiescence toward the pun and the decorative. Puns and quips are not for my drawing. When I use them I feel as if the image were saying back to me:

> Some distances between organ and interval are sacred.
> Some proportion between irascible wit and devout love is to be maintained.
> A nose belongs fatally where it is. Likewise the heart. The same with the eyes, including sight and excluding fancy views.
> There is a point past which nipples reduced to penpoints do not nurse, because calligraphy, alone, is a sterile spinster.

THE FUNDAMENTALS

The fundamentals of drawing are the fundamentals of active passion.

Lebrun

24

In teaching, we neglect to sponsor passion as a discipline. The only discipline we teach is that of the deadly diagram supposedly to be fertilized later by personal experience. Later is too late.

The canonical points of structure are in us, but we have become totally inert in sensing this presence. Discipline intervenes and deals with them as if they were strangers to be captured by skillful ruses. Thus a game of stalking results rather than a dialogue with the self, which is all form.

There is a kind of rendering which is a lie, which is coming to terms with the image by dusting it with respectful attention. The live image is a tiger. To rearrange his crossed paws and roll him on his back is more like true drawing than anything I know.

Even the slightest indication must at all costs avoid vagueness. The writing must be intense and specific. The blocking in of large masses, simulating boldness, is often a promissory note which we will not be able to honor later. It is, in fact, the story of the particular which leads properly to the general. A false reading of the particular will change the entire structure. If the range of a kneecap were made of octagonal bones in equidistant arrangement from a central point, our *total* looks would be vastly different. Grünewald's arms grew from the web of arterial net to the surface, yet not as anatomy but as a river commanding the nature of the terrain. In him the minute and the particular are the true lead to the eccentric unfolding of form, the opening of the bivalve shapes, the uncoiling of a map full of relevance.

25

In reality all forms are in foreshortening, never adhering to the fiction of plane; so are all events. True drawing is a suspended state of animation, a temporary conquest of the mobile shape. Line functions as sandbanks do in a flood, according to the pressure of emergency.

Because we are numb about the facts of the world, we are timid about giving them presence even on the small field of the page. Simultaneous and resolute survey (that is, encompassing the figure from all sides at once), the only natural gesture possible in drawing, baffles us. Thus we do strange things. For instance, we who walk the earth constantly start the drawing of a standing figure at the top of the page. Why not from the ground up—or for that matter, why not from the heart out?

Lebrun

26

Foot was root. Loin was valley. Breasts were solstices. Head, eclipse. Eyes, wells tearful. Jaw, bridge suspended. Ear, leaf carnivorous. Guts, lace meander. Weight was will to lower, contested by earth horizontal. Hair was tornado turning. Mouth, pomegranate burning. Heartbeat notwithstanding, he sat down and made a drawing.

Gutter was sunlit urine. Wall was mimosa in flower. Pater detested mother. Infant was mocking stranger. Words were to be forgotten. Womb to humiliate lover. Usual was in power. Birds were impeded messengers. Anguish had her hair in curlers. Teacher was deflowering pupil. Heartbeat notwithstanding, he sat down and made a drawing.

People were leaving forever. Songs could afford no rhymer. Gender was confused by spelling. Meaning was treble and fearful. General had given the signal. Town was a burning brazier. Infant was screaming siren. Heartbeat notwithstanding, he sat down.

EXECUTION OF A FIGURE

She appeared on the canvas with a will of her own and damned near clouted me. She was an awful cage full of crows. Decorum had flown out, and the melon-titted mantis was tear-jerked and kaput. I tried to redesign her, but she kept breaking away from any sustained gesture I could impose with the rictus of a screaming hen. I could have settled everything with a *bel canto* outline, but she unraveled it and tossed it off like a cobweb. I proposed some kind of mutual forbearance; I solicited her to appear. She refused in spite of the thirty years of *solfeggio* I have at my command. My eloquence had nothing to do with her need. She was nothing to be executed. She was executing a foolish painter. Fortunate the nursing baby who can be so at one with her without the frenzied sadness of lust.

How much more expedient to dismiss her as a subject. But if I did so, to become free, I would be an orphan, which is the most awful of free things in the world.

DRAWING

"My little line takes a walk," said Klee.

"As if mine didn't," said Tintoretto.

True, lines do not exist in nature; we invent them. They are poetic fiction. The line is a thing unto itself. Then why not dismiss the object and make line the main actor? Because without the impediment of experience, line can only perform capers.

You see it everywhere now—the indication, the note, the perhaps, the maybe, the drawing non-drawing, the now-you-see-it, now-you-don't; the big adventure in which line being a widow of the dead object takes a little walk by herself and, after a sad meeting with the plane, comes back home in excellent bloom because nothing whatever happened to her, neither rape nor love. It was when she coincided with necessity that she was leaner and more of a real bedfellow. Nowadays, pure and free, she has no dates and no bleedings. I think she can be alive again, a murderess, a calamity, a delight, anything but this fearful pretense at self-sufficiency.

I shun drawing which is too easily formulated. It does not seem fertilized enough to produce consequences, and a drawing should be a provoker of consequences. It should be, above all, not a thing of art but a tool for understanding. I wish my drawing to get richer by consulting the tangible world. I am just beginning to see how even the most static form is bounded by profiles so constantly changing that the form itself is in movement. This inherent animation, which has nothing to do with action, offers me a chance to select and transfer to the paper those contours which most fully describe that movement and that life. When I become arbitrary in my selection, the drawing weakens; it is at this point that elegance, spontaneity, and freshness often take over and essentially destroy meaning.

The fine edge between the pertinent and the brilliant can be maintained only with the greatest effort. On the other hand, the deceptively simple means of line can lead time and again to half-truths. Seemingly the most easy of all crafts, drawing is the one which reveals most tellingly our incapacity to sustain true vision and our acquiescence to the ready-made. This baffling fact has haunted the work of even some of the greatest master draftsmen. And the nature of the task has all along been so strenuous that it is easy to see why drawing in our own time has moved violently away from the contest with the ascertainable world. Not only did it not want to repeat the results of the masters of the past (a moral resolution to be fully endorsed), but it could not find symbols of its own potent enough to equal in validity what tradition had already achieved. And in trying to find a new world of its own, the line—living into itself, disengaging itself more and more—finally achieved an ironical independence which is fine to see but not nourishing to the soul.

SCALE

If anyone had told Ahab that the tidal pool at his feet contained a microcosm of the drama of many waters and that he need go no further, he would have brushed the speaker out of the way and gone about his business, which was the meeting with that full-sized, life-sized baroque excrescence, Moby-Dick. And because I am on the side of Ahab, I would feel physically ill at ease in depicting a miniature whale—a whale you can hold in the palm of your hand, a leviathan you can hang in the parlor, surrounded by inches of green signifying the raging salt. Insane reduction; to me truly a repellent abstraction. I know that this problem of general and specific scale has its humorous side. But nature itself is humorous when it proposes the sardine beside the cetacean or the leviathan. Jonah as a draftsman describing

Lebrun

28

the whale would have chosen the scale which was as vast as his predicament. This may well mean that the preference many of us have for the monumental is not a whim.

CRUCIFIXION

After Christ was taken down and the Golgotha scaffold scrubbed with whitewash, someone discovered that without the irrelevant trivia of blood and pain the Cross made a composition of "significant horizontals and verticals."

This meant nothing at all to Mary the Mother. Her sight had been made unsophisticated by experience.

To me the repetition of the symbol of the Crucifixion comes as a necessary act; I can thus make its daily immanence real and present. We try to ignore this presence; we say that it is a fable of times past. Meanwhile thousands are being destroyed by malice and terror every day.

As for art in the churches of today, look at what vapid things are condoned by the ecclesiastic mind. With few gallant exceptions, one of the most potent systems of abstract thought which ever bridged the terrestial to the heavenly, the Christian dogma, is at the lowest ebb of the innocuous in art. Being Christian by birth and choice, I still have a hundred versions of the Calvary to do, in the shape of prayer, in all forms and colors; from the imperceptible white of first agony to the ultimate hues which transfigured the gibbet. Repetitive in design, the crosses span the terrain of all experience, repetitive as our zest to nail others with the tongue if not the hammer.

THE MODEL

I find it best to work from objects and the figure literally, then to continue in the same stride, working away from model or object but still fresh from the contact with them. But it is not until the drawing assumes the look of a protest against the fetters of dictation from the object, and breathes a definite air of controlled deliverance, that I feel perfectly at home and totally involved. I keep telling myself that the line should finally look as if traced with a full sense of life, not traced *from* life. As a matter of fact I cannot think of a single master of line who does not seem to exemplify this in his work. A master's drawing seems periodically to reach this state of a free "second wind" which affirms the total image with something over and above what he usually knows. The best moments of technique are those in which it surpasses expectations because it is fed up with them.

In executing I endeavor to complete a drawing in one single, continuous gesture. However, far from trying to be selective and impeccable, I write down forms over and over again in a sort of animated framework, never tentatively but as fully as possible. The rehearsal is conducted, so to speak, with full phrases and not single sounds.

Lebrun

30

ON WORKING FROM GOYA

Occasionally I like to select a mentor, a master, and let him guide me through a revision of one of his paintings. When I do this I forgo for a time the option of taking on nature or my own images and I adopt the image of some other man. Periodically I need to take sustenance in this way. By either understanding or misunderstanding lyrically—which is my right to do—his basic intentions, I try to see how much I can transform what he did. I try to move into his terrain, bringing my own ammunition.

I do not believe by even the most pious stretch of conscience that this belittles my own personality. It seems to me that, as in music, to take a theme already in existence and to write meaningful variations on this theme is one of the most challenging tasks an artist can face. Not mechanically and not as a virtuoso manifestation of daring, but because there are certain themes in paint—or words, or notes—which lend themselves to fresh reading and consequent new discoveries.

THE CHILD AND THE MAN

No one at the age of six ever made drawings like the mature Raphael or Picasso of the *Guernica*. *Guernica* is to be six at fifty, which is another story.

At the age of six I could make only those magnificent passes at the paper which later, contested by existence, shrink into their proper role of unfulfilled portents. The promises of that Eden are so ample they become diffuse, they vanish. The child draftsman is an unconscious fourflusher, and when life pushes him around he gives up. The master does not, and that is the difference. All great drawing is made by the strategy of innocence, with the ammunition of adulthood. Let us then not talk about Eden but about Purgatory made manageable by experience, which is technique.

Words are fiction, and we could let it go at that if sometimes they did not counter exactly what facts say. I am thinking of the two words "early" and "late," often used in discussing the work of an artist. As I look at my drawings it seems quite clear that the early ones are often very late in time, a corollary to many masters' drawings, in spite of the fact that they are not indifferent or lacking in sentiment or weight. As I have proceeded, my wish has been to make them more surprisingly new, "early," as early as tomorrow, for me to find and to recognize them. They are more of the lost and found and of the unrehearsed kind. New, they do not quite know how to turn and place themselves. I encourage them to appear, but often they are reticent to take the proscenium of the page or the footlight. Thus I now prefer the conduct and the execution of a drawing to be precarious, slow, weighted, almost unhinged by relevance, loaded with more responsibility. Responsibility toward what? Toward themselves as images. The page can be the map for a conducted tour or a flood of the heart, and in the charts of these are, of course, the difference between the contrived and the expressed.

That sustained quality, that writing of the continuous cipher of the body, or of the rock, or of the sky, as if with a letter (someday I will have the A's and the B's and the C's of general anatomy), is to me nowadays best when *not* in the character of a breeze, but more like an unequal and stubborn blast, through and around the impediments of the terrain. The terrain should not concede easily; the line should persist in its survey, with measured passion. Give and take, that's it; as in everything else, that's the real business.

After you have covered literally miles with a moving line you get closer to the point of execution, which either starts from your viscera to extend and deploy you as a spectacle and a composition or is not worth starting at all. Too many drawings, mine and others' alike, are outlines and not journeys. I have done my share in destroying reams of them. Not everything we put down deserves the honor, particularly when competence makes it almost good by leaning on what we knew yesterday.

I think that in trying to have them come into this world naked and revealed I have systematically stripped the flesh from my figures— a strange resolution if you will, in graphic terms, a doing away with the impedimenta. Thus they seemed to me more consumed. They are not depicting emaciation as much as the leaner, the more permanent geography of the body. In the death drawings I am not a necrophile— I simply have a kind of solicitude for what remains, survives. At this stage the drawing is no longer carnal but Christian.

THE SKETCH

When we cannot really talk we gossip. When we cannot draw we "sketch," hoping to bypass the difficult through brevity.

Considering the nature of the true sketch, it is remarkable that so many use it without understanding the character of the engagement. Sketching is the shorthand of the language of drawing; the language is almost universally unknown.

The sketch should be the unerring chart of a condition. It should never be used temporarily to placate vanity, which seeks to affirm itself through the delusion of promises made and promptly forgotten. Anxiety can encourage vacillation to suggest promising but untenable hints. It can lead you to shoot a round of ammunition at an imaginary target while the enemy is sitting on your rudder. It can reassure for the wrong reasons.

The precision of a real sketch is directly arrived at according to the general climate of the day. We know that the secretary of state, reports on alcohol, dope, and polio vaccine, and the trends of general hope or collective malevolence can and must intervene in the making of a sketch. Even when only the size of a thumbnail, the sketch cannot avoid submitting to these factors. Line, of course, participates to the utmost degree. But the motions of the hand must come from much further up than the elbow. Line will alter its course as it proceeds, according to what the ticker tape of these combined portents says from minute to minute. *Do not use calligraphic barrel rolls in combat.* They are not organic. *Do not gun the engine when you don't know what else to do.*

If true to its mission or fate the sketch will be from day to day catastrophic or hopeful, stampeded or united, explosive and equivocal (as in baroque art), or formal and adamant against calamity (as in classical art). Only one rule can be safely followed in its execution: be prepared not to do at all today what you did yesterday.

Grünewald's secret system, or "How to Draw at Home through Correspondence"

> The rock the belly the toad the hand
> A webbed and pronged world appear
> The eye can summon and disband
> Through a crystal tear.

Withal, I never seem to have time enough to do what I wish. The day is never long enough, and daylight slow to come. I love black, but the best blacks with the most meaning can be done only in full light of day—noontime blacks. Dark vision demands its own clarity. I am never agitated in executing forms, but travel rather as if the terrain of the paper was land-mined. When this journey is completed, a drawing is born.

Lebrun

34

Drawings

1. *Figure in Dust Storm   1936*
   Collection of Santa Barbara Museum of Art
   Gift of the Honorable and Mrs. Robert Woods Bliss

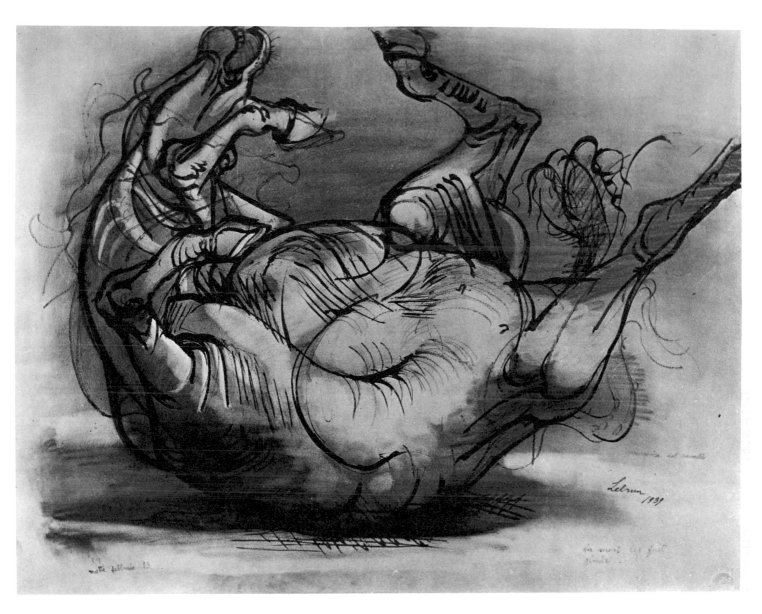

2. *Thus He Died 1939*
Collection of Mr. Hugh J. Chisholm, Jr.

3. *Portrait of Kate Lawson   1940*
   Collection of Mr. and Mrs. M. F. Feheley

4. *Portrait of a Man*   *1941*
Private collection

5. *Clown   1941*
   Collection of Santa Barbara Museum of Art
   Gift of Mr. and Mrs. Arthur B. Sachs

6. *Eroica 1941*
Collection of Mrs. Guenn Farrington

7. *Woman Leaning on a Staff   1941*
   Collection of Mr. and Mrs. Thomas A. Freiberg

8. *Night 1942*
Private collection

9. *Massacre of the Innocents   1948*
   Collection of Mr. and Mrs. Bernard Comsky

10. *Roman Soldier Asleep with Flower in His Ear   1948*
Collection of Mr. and Mrs. Silvan Simone

11. *Woman of the Crucifixion   1948*
    Collection of Mr. and Mrs. Ross R. DeVean

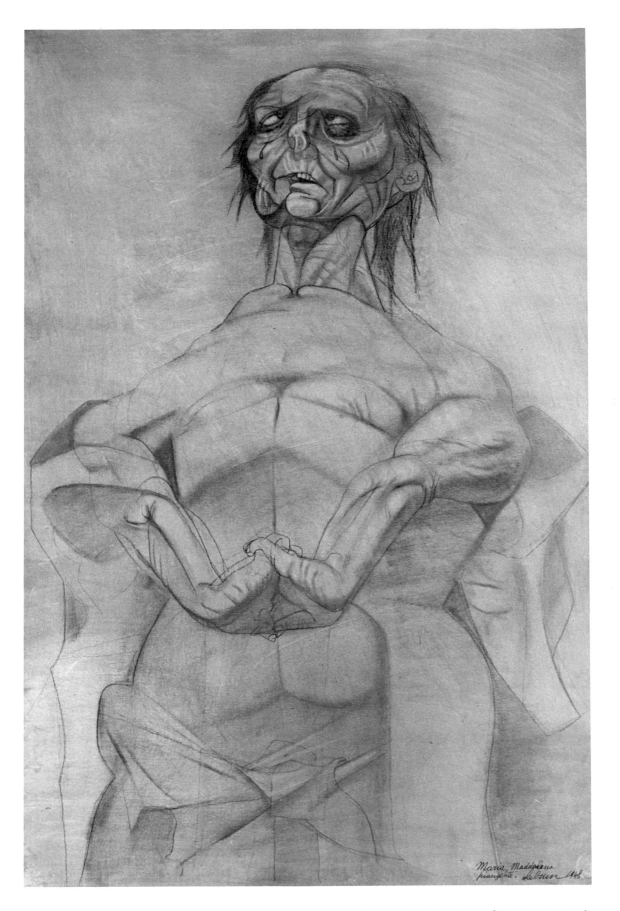

12. *Woman of the Crucifixion (Maria Magdalena)* *1948*
Collection of Mr. and Mrs. Vincent Price

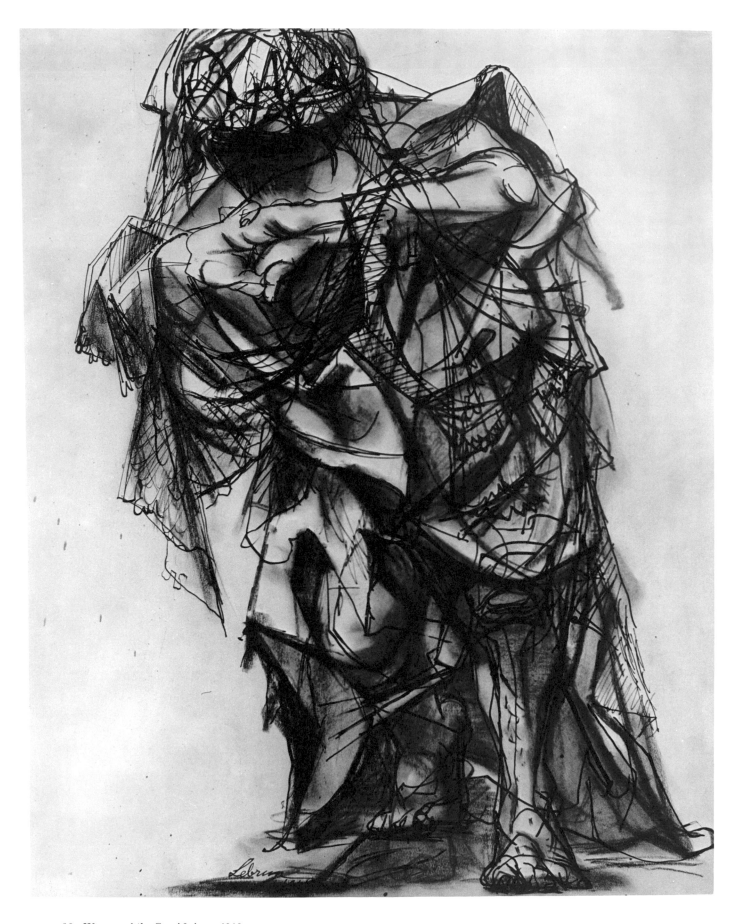

13. *Woman of the Crucifixion   1948*
     Collection of Constance Lebrun

14. *Running Woman with Child   1948*
Collection of Whitney Museum of American Art

15. *Soldiers with Flares   1949*
    Collection of Dr. and Mrs. Marvin J. Shapiro

16. *Carpenter on the Cross with Lantern   1950*
Collection of Mr. and Mrs. Harold P. Ullman

17. *Scene of the Crucifixion   1950*
    Collection of Victoria and David Thorne

18. *Woman of the Crucifixion 1950*
Collection of Mr. Channing Peake

19. *Woman of the Crucifixion   1950*
    Private collection

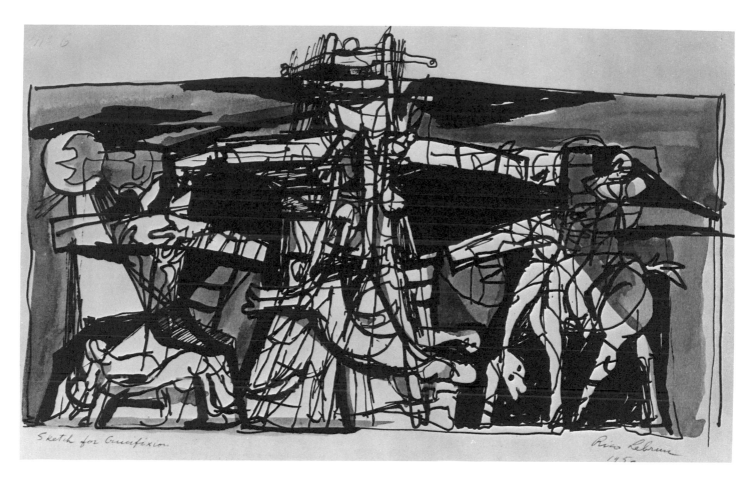

Sketch for Crucifixion

Rico Lebrun
195-

20. *Scene of the Crucifixion   1950*
Collection of Constance Lebrun

21. *Soldiers with Flares*   *1950*
   Collection of the artist

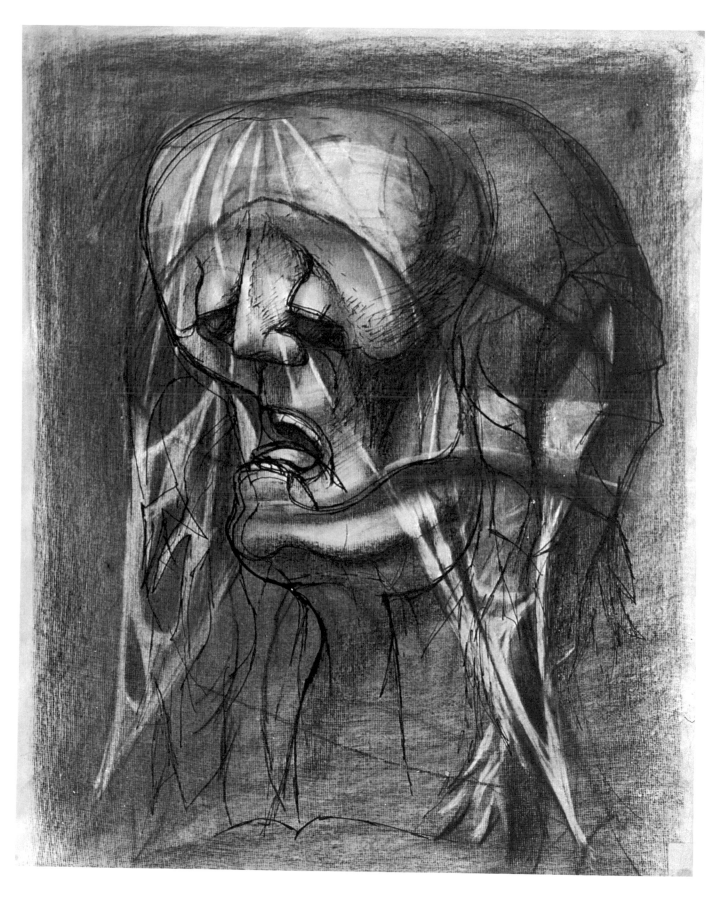

22. Head of Woman of the Crucifixion 1950
Collection of Miss Georgia R. Vester

23. *Soldiers with Flares* 1950
    Collection of the artist

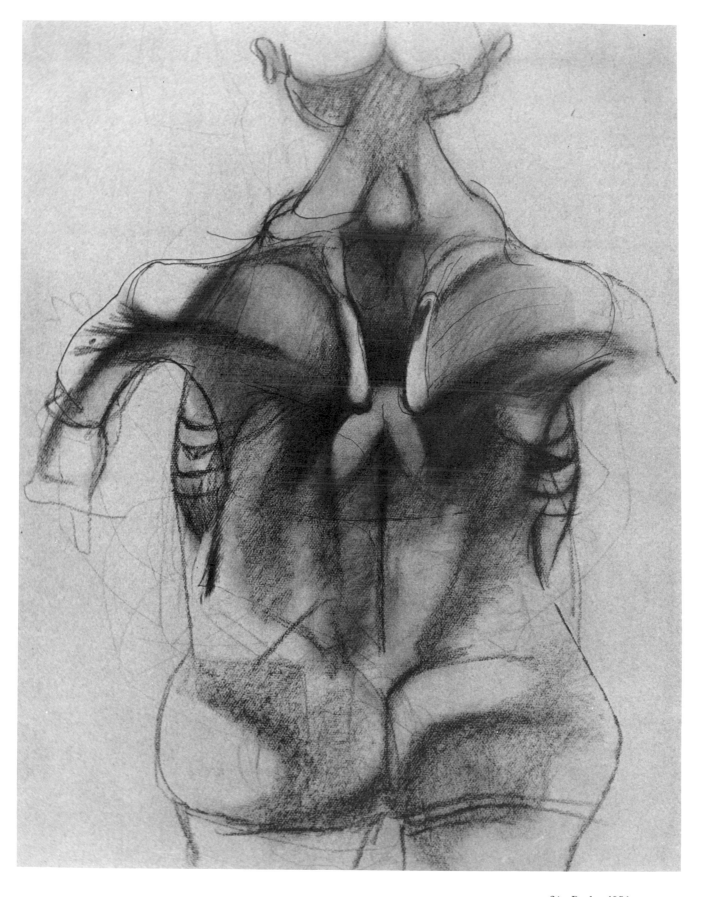

24. *Back* 1951
Collection of the artist

25. *Grieving Figures   1953*
   Collection of Mr. and Mrs. David Mellinkoff

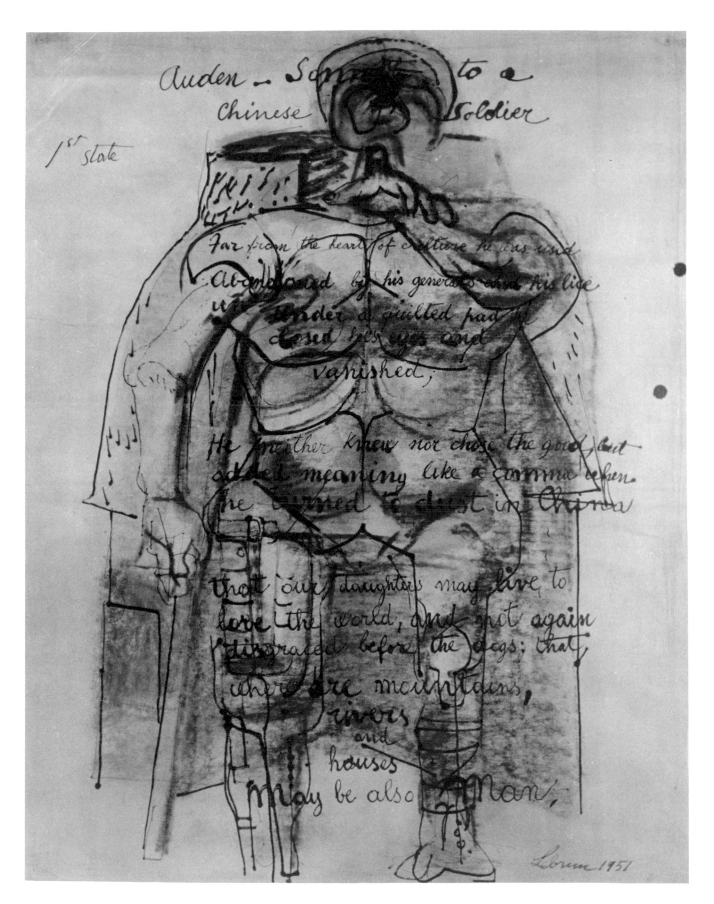

26. *Drawing for a Poem by Auden   1951*
Collection of Mr. and Mrs. Stuart E. Weaver, Jr.

Pilar, nuda.

Lebrun
1954

27. *Pilar Nuda   1954*
    Collection of Mr. and Mrs. Leonard Titelman

28. *Magdalen and Centurion   1956*
Collection of Constance Lebrun

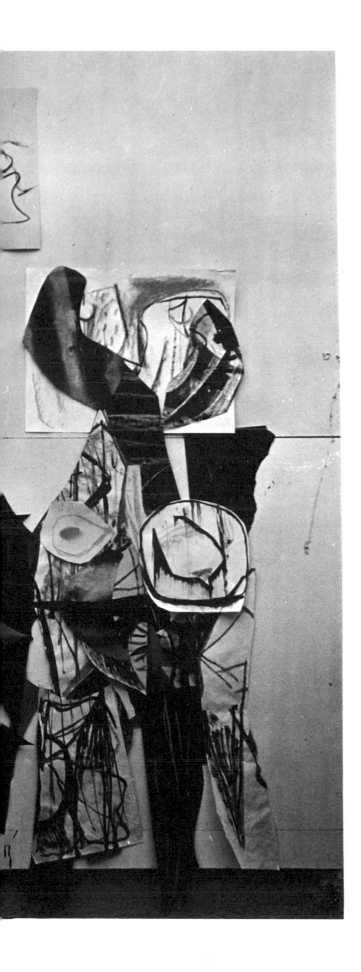

29. *Crucifixion 1954*
Later disassembled

30. *Buchenwald Pit* 1956
Collection of the artist

31. *Members of the Resurrection 1957*
   Collection of Mr. and Mrs. Robert W. Pethick

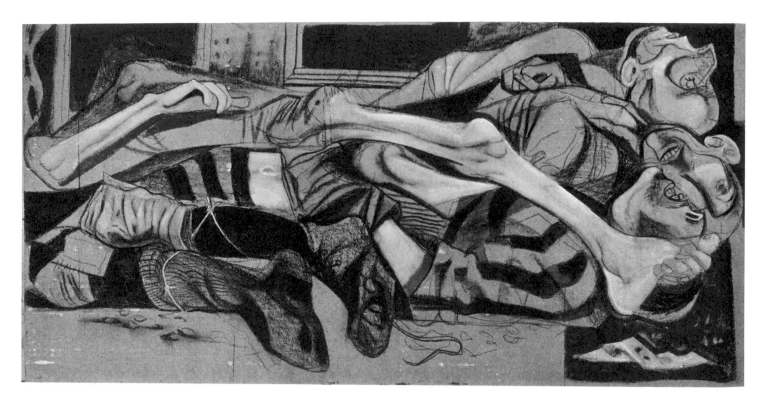

32. *Floor of Buchenwald #1   1957*
    Collection of the artist

33. *Floor of Buchenwald #2   1957*
   Collection of the artist

34. *Dachau   1958*
    Collection of the artist

35. *Disparate Matrimonial (from Goya)* *1957*
Collection of Mr. and Mrs. Barry Kernerman

36. *Mule and Goat (Goyesca)*   *1957*
   Collection of Mr. and Mrs. Sumner Gerstein

37. *Tauromachy 1957*
Collection of the artist

38. *Lovers* 1957
   Collection of the artist

39. *Familia Real   1958*
Collection of Mr. and Mrs. Joel Grey

40. *Maria Luisa (after Goya)*   *1958*
     Collection of the artist

41. *Reclining Nude 1957*
Collection of the artist

42. *Sunflowers 1957*
   Collection of Dr. and Mrs. Wallace Graham

43. *Portrait of Teresa*   *1958*
Collection of the artist

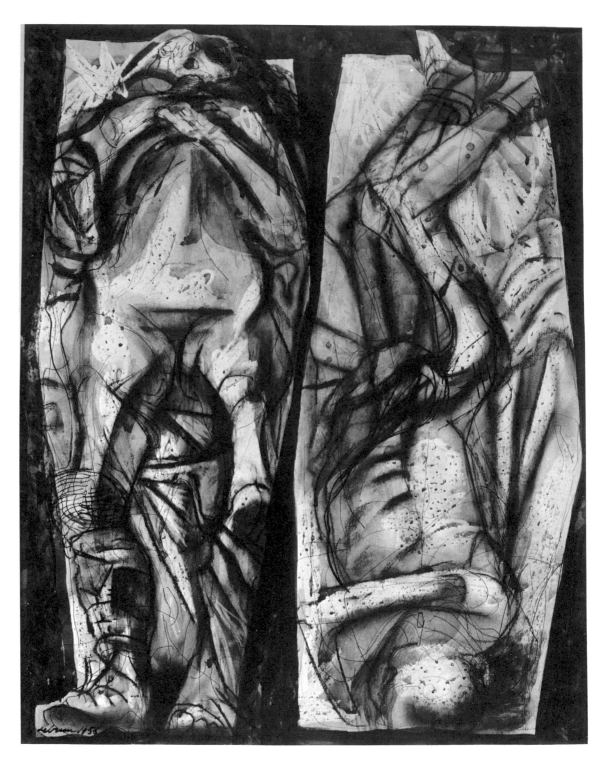

44. *Members of the Resurrection   1958*
   Collection of Mr. Robert Service

45. *Crucifixion   1958*
Collection of the artist

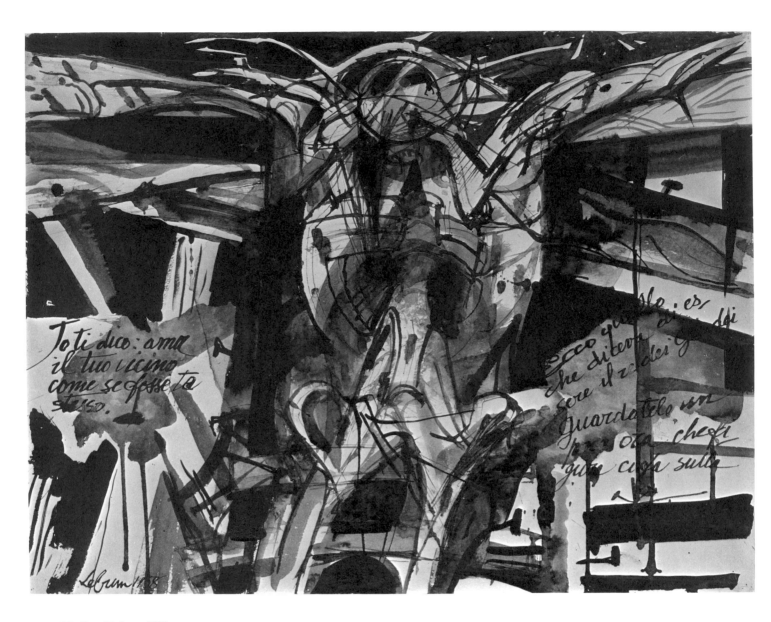

46. *Crucifixion   1958*
   Collection of the artist

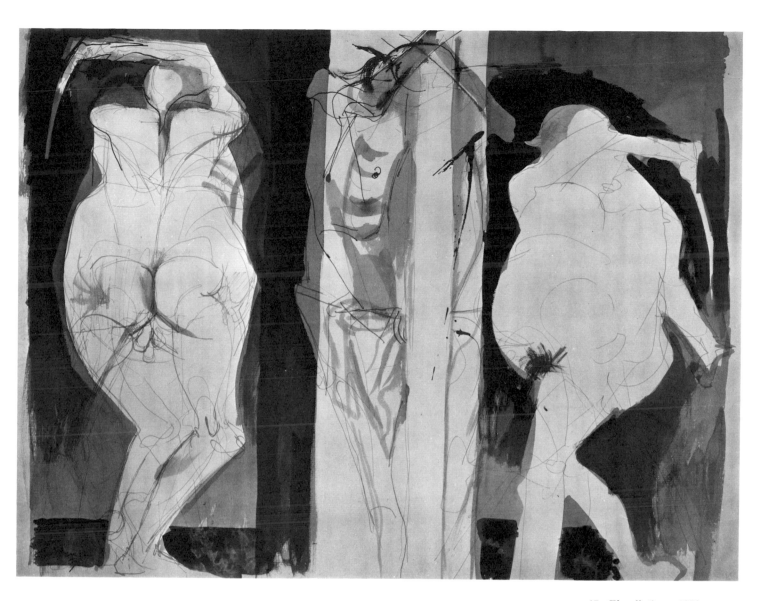

47. *Flagellation 1959*
Collection of the artist

48. *Two Women Disrobing   1959*
    Collection of the artist

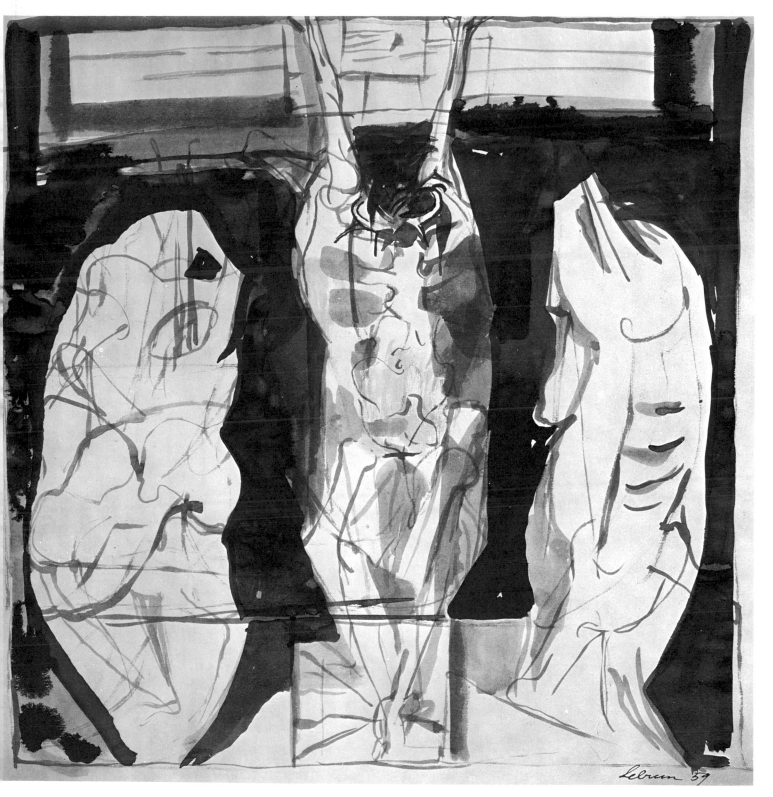

Lebrun 59

49. *Crucifixion* *1959*
Collection of the artist

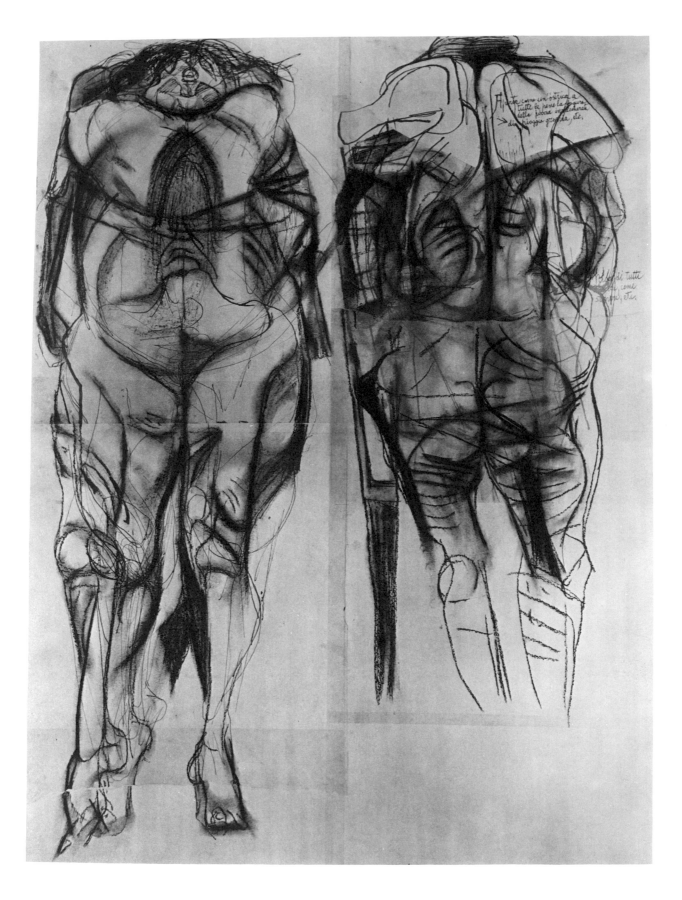

50. *Two Standing Figures   1959*
    Collection of the artist

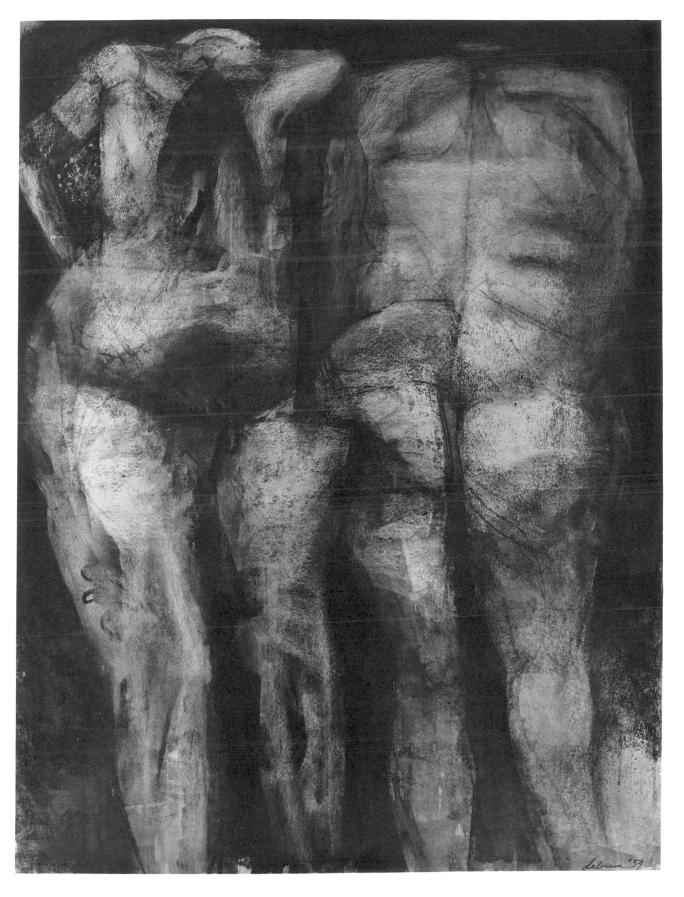

51. *Two Standing Figures   1959*
Collection of Mr. and Mrs. M. F. Feheley

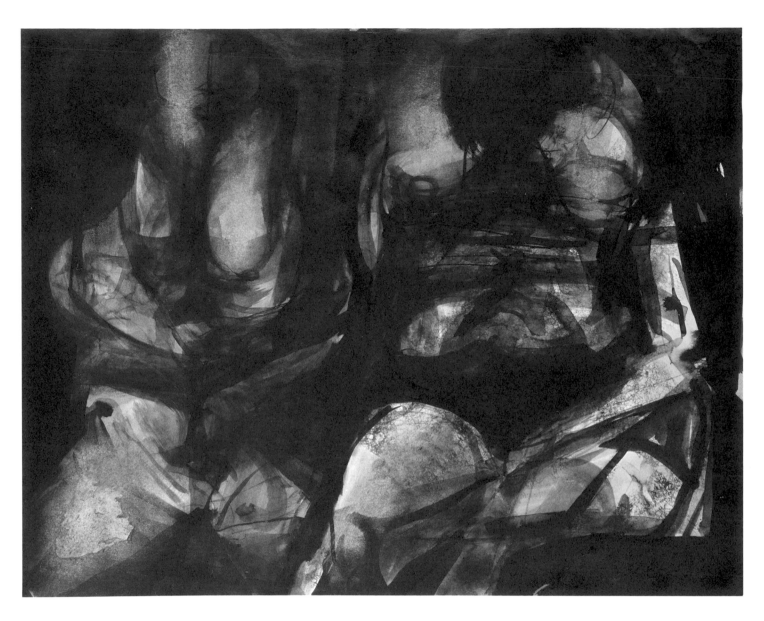

52. *Two Sitting Figures at Night   1959*
   Collection of the artist

53. *Casualties   1959*
Collection of the artist

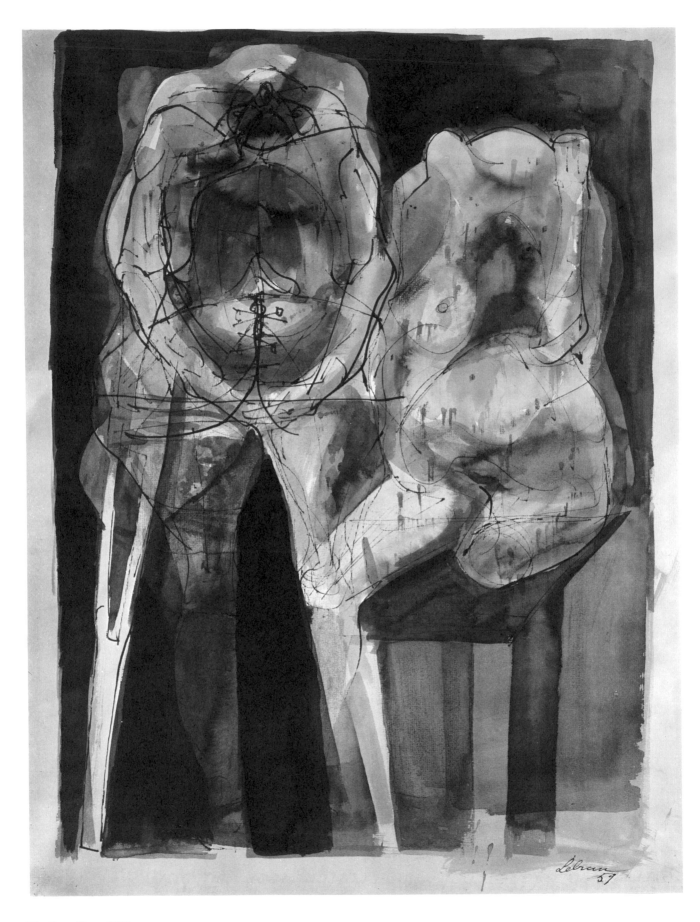

54. *Casualties 1959*
Collection of the artist

55. *Crowd* *1959*
Collection of the artist

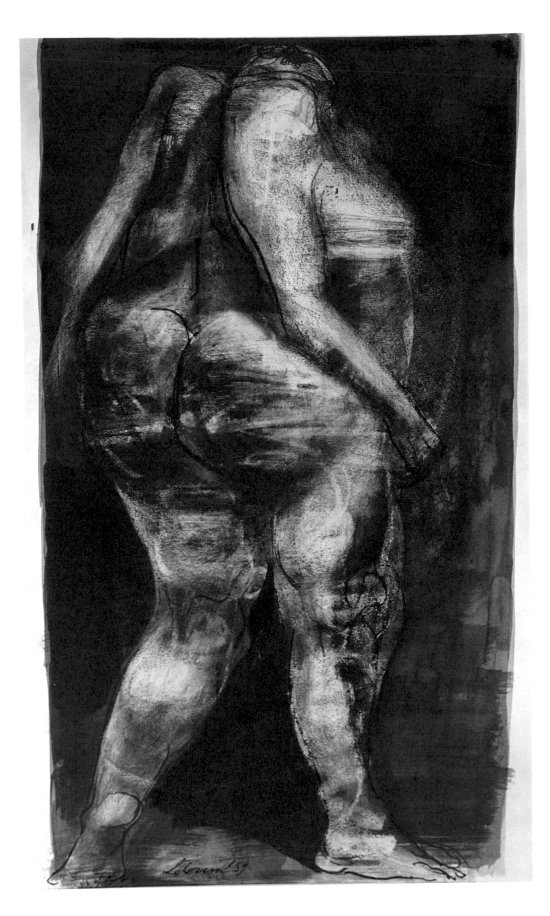

56. *Standing Figure   1959*
   Collection of Mr. Nathaniel Saltonstall

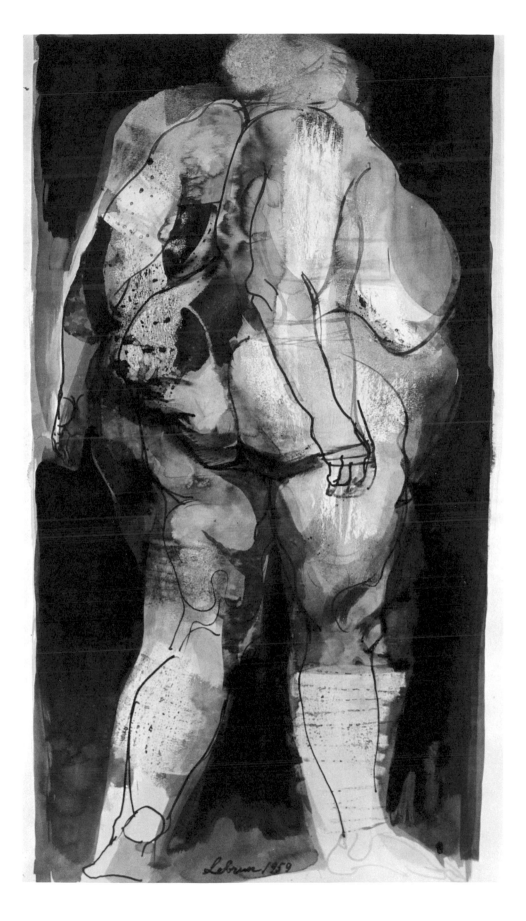

57. *Figure with Bandaged Legs 1959*
Collection of Miss Adele Clement

58. *Casualties   1959*
   Collection of William H. Lane Foundation

Catalog of Drawings

Catalog of Drawings

1. *Figure in Dust Storm 1936*
   Ink and chalk
   24⅛ x 18
   Collection of Santa Barbara
   Museum of Art
   Gift of the Honorable and
   Mrs. Robert Woods Bliss

2. *Thus He Died 1939*
   Ink and chalk
   28 x 34
   Collection of Mr. Hugh J.
   Chisholm, Jr.

3. *Portrait of Kate Lawson 1940*
   Ink and chalk
   Collection of Mr. and
   Mrs. M. F. Feheley

4. *Portrait of a Man 1941*
   Ink and chalk
   Private collection

5. *Clown 1941*
   Ink and chalk
   39½ x 29
   Collection of Santa Barbara
   Museum of Art
   Gift of Mr. and Mrs.
   Arthur B. Sachs

6. *Eroica 1941*
   Ink and chalk
   26 x 19
   Collection of
   Mrs. Guenn Farrington

7. *Woman Leaning on a Staff 1941*
   Ink and chalk
   25¼ x 11¼
   Collection of Mr. and Mrs.
   Thomas A. Freiberg

8. *Night 1942*
   Pencil
   19 x 25
   Private collection

9. *Massacre of the Innocents 1948*
   Ink and chalk
   19 x 25
   Collection of Mr. and Mrs.
   Bernard Comsky

10. *Roman Soldier Asleep with Flower*
    in His Ear 1948
    Pen and ink
    16 x 24
    Collection of Mr. and Mrs.
    Silvan Simone

11. *Woman of the Crucifixion 1948*
    Ink, chalk, and casein
    40 x 30
    Collection of Mr. and Mrs.
    Ross R. DeVean

12. *Woman of the Crucifixion (Maria*
    Magdalena) 1948
    Ink and chalk 29 x 19½
    Collection of Mr. and Mrs.
    Vincent Price

13. *Woman of the Crucifixion   1948*
    Chalk and ink
    24 x 19
    Collection of Constance Lebrun

14. *Running Woman with Child   1948*
    Ink wash
    19 x 25
    Collection of Whitney Museum of
        American Art

15. *Soldiers with Flares   1949*
    Ink wash
    12½ x 19½
    Collection of Dr. and Mrs.
        Marvin J. Shapiro

16. *Carpenter on the Cross with*
        Lantern   1950
    Ink and chalk
    20 x 26
    Collection of Mr. and Mrs.
        Harold P. Ullman

17. *Scene of the Crucifixion   1950*
    Ink wash
    14 x 27½
    Collection of Victoria and
        David Thorne

18. *Woman of the Crucifixion*
    1950
    Ink and chalk
    12 x 7¼
    Collection of Mr.
        Channing Peake

19. *Woman of the Crucifixion*
    1950
    Ink and chalk
    12 x 7¼
    Private collection

20. *Scene of the Crucifixion   1950*
    Ink wash
    Collection of Constance Lebrun

21. *Soldiers with Flares   1950*
    Ink wash
    38 x 51
    Collection of the artist

22. *Head of Woman of the*
        Crucifixion   1950
    Ink and chalk
    23 x 17
    Collection of Miss
        Georgia R. Vester

23. *Soldiers with Flares   1950*
    Ink and chalk
    7 x 11
    Collection of the artist

24. *Back   1951*
    Ink and chalk
    25 x 19
    Collection of the artist

25. *Grieving Figures   1953*
    Collage
    77½ x 39
    Collection of Mr. and Mrs.
        David Mellinkoff

26. *Drawing for a Poem by Auden*
        1951
    Ink and chalk
    30 x 24
    Collection of Mr. and Mrs.
        Stuart E. Weaver, Jr.

27. *Pilar Nuda   1954*
    Ink wash and charcoal
    22½ x 17⅜
    Collection of Mr. and Mrs.
        Leonard Titelman

28. *Magdalen and Centurion   1956*
    Collage
    42 x 78
    Collection of Constance Lebrun

29. *Crucifixion   1954*
    Collage (later disassembled)

30. *Buchenwald Pit   1956*
    Charcoal on canvas
    80¼ x 98
    Collection of the artist

31. *Members of the Resurrection   1957*
    Ink wash
    22½ x 28½
    Collection of Mr. and Mrs.
        Robert W. Pethick

32. *Floor of Buchenwald #1   1957*
    Casein and ink
    48 x 96
    Collection of the artist

33. *Floor of Buchenwald #2   1957*
    Casein and ink
    48 x 96
    Collection of the artist

34. *Dachau   1958*
    Ink on canvas
    75 x 86
    Collection of the artist

35. *Disparate Matrimonial*
      (from Goya)   1957
    31⅞ x 26¾
    Collection of Mr. and Mrs.
      Barry Kernerman

36. *Mule and Goat (Goyesca)   1957*
    Ink wash
    25 x 18½
    Collection of Mr. and Mrs.
      Sumner Gerstein

37. *Tauromachy   1957*
    Ink wash and collage
    28½ x 22½
    Collection of the artist

38. *Lovers   1957*
    Ink wash
    28¾ x 20½
    Collection of the artist

39. *Familia Real   1958*
    Ink on board
    61 x 40
    Collection of Mr. and Mrs.
      Joel Grey

40. *Maria Luisa (after Goya)   1958*
    Ink wash
    86½ x 36
    Collection of the artist

41. *Reclining Nude   1957*
    Ink wash
    19 x 25
    Collection of the artist

42. *Sunflowers   1957*
    Ink wash
    29 x 20½
    Collection of Dr. and Mrs.
      Wallace Graham

43. *Portrait of Teresa   1958*
    Charcoal on canvas
    72 x 54
    Collection of the artist

44. *Members of the Resurrection   1958*
    Wash, ink, and wax
    28½ x 22½
    Collection of Mr. Robert Service

45. *Crucifixion   1958*
    Ink wash
    23 x 29
    Collection of the artist

46. *Crucifixion   1958*
    Ink wash
    20 x 25½
    Collection of the artist

47. *Flagellation   1959*
    Ink wash
    19 x 25
    Collection of the artist

99

48. *Two Women Disrobing   1959*
    Ink wash
    19 x 25
    Collection of the artist

49. *Crucifixion   1959*
    Ink wash
    18 x 17¼
    Collection of the artist

50. *Two Standing Figures   1959*
    Ink and chalk on tracing paper
    60½ x 41
    Collection of the artist

51. *Two Standing Figures   1959*
    Ink wash and wax
    40 x 30
    Collection of Mr. and Mrs.
    M. F. Feheley

52. *Two Sitting Figures at Night 1959*
    Ink wash
    22½ x 29
    Collection of the artist

53. *Casualties   1959*
    Ink wash
    24 x 18
    Collection of the artist

54. *Casualties   1959*
    Ink wash
    23½ x 17
    Collection of the artist

55. *Crowd   1959*
    Ink wash
    19 x 25
    Collection of the artist

56. *Standing Figure   1959*
    Ink wash and wax
    30 x 16
    Collection of Mr. Nathaniel
    Saltonstall

57. *Figure with Bandaged Legs   1959*
    Ink wash and wax
    30 x 15¾
    Collection of Miss Adele Clement

58. *Casualties   1959*
    Ink wash and wax
    22 x 30
    Collection of William H. Lane
    Foundation

100

---

title page.
   Sitting Nude   1958
   Charcoal and ink
   24¾ x 19
   Collection of Mr.
   Selden Rodman

p. 2. *Woman   1959*
   Ink wash
   20⅜ x 28¼
   Collection of the artist

p. 7. *The Ragged One   1941*
   Ink and chalk
   28 x 22
   Collection of Mrs. Elsie Rieti

p. 13. Rooster on the Arm of the Cross
   1950
   Ink wash
   15 x 40
   Collection of Constance Lebrun

p. 17. Project for a Wall   1959
   Ink wash
   28¼ x 20⅜
   Collection of the artist

p. 22. Horsemen in Cemetery   1959
   Ink wash
   27 x 20⅜
   Collection of the artist

p. 27. Hands   1946
   Pen and ink
   19 x 25
   Collection of Dr. and Mrs.
   Sidney D. Leo

p. 31. Scene of the Crucifixion   1950
   Ink wash
   7½ x 18½
   Collection of Miss Florita Botts